CHOCOLATE

Jacqueline Dineen

Illustrations by John Yates

Carolrhoda Books, Inc./Minneapolis

All words that appear in **bold** are
explained in the glossary on page 30.

First published in the U.S. in 1991 by
Carolrhoda Books, Inc.

Library of Congress Cataloging-in-Publication Data

Dineen, Jacqueline.
    Chocolate / Jacqueline Dineen ; illustrations by John Yates.
        p.   cm.
    Includes index.
    Summary: Discusses the role of chocolate in history, where it
comes from, and how it is processed and prepared for eating.
    ISBN 0-87614-657-4
    1. Cookery (Chocolate)—Juvenile literature. 2. Cocoa—Juvenile
literature. 3. Chocolate—Juvenile literature. [1. Chocolcate.]
I. Yates, John, 1939- ill. II. Title
TX767.C5D56   1990
641.6'374—dc20   90-46422
                                                                      CIP
                                                                       AC

Printed in Italy by G. Canale & C.S.p.A., Turin
Bound in the United States of America

1 2 3 4 5 6 7 8 9 10 00 99 98 97 96 95 94 93 92 91

Contents

What is chocolate?   4

The history of chocolate   6

Where does chocolate come from?   10

Growing cacao trees   12

Harvesting cacao beans   14

From farm to factory   16

Making cocoa powder   18

Making chocolate   20

Chocolate and your body   22

Cooking with chocolate   24

Chocolate crispies   26

Brownies   27

Chocolate cake   28

Glossary   30

Index   32

What is chocolate?

Almost everyone likes chocolate. How many foods made with chocolate can you think of? There are chocolate bars and boxes of chocolate candies. There are chocolate-chip cookies and chocolate brownies, chocolate-frosted cakes and chocolate pudding, chocolate ice cream and even chocolate cereal. The chocolate itself may be the dark or milk variety. Chocolate is popular in most parts of the world, and it is used in many different ways.

Do you know how chocolate is made? Both dark and milk chocolate start as beans growing in pods on **cacao trees**. The dried cacao beans are then roasted and ground, and **cocoa butter** is released. The main ingredient in chocolate is **chocolate liquor**, a mixture of cocoa butter and ground cacao beans.

The history of chocolate

Cacao trees grow wild in the tropical climates of South and Central America. Long before Europeans traveled to the Americas, the Incas in Peru and the Aztecs in Mexico had discovered that cacao beans could be roasted to bring out the chocolate flavor. They crushed the roasted beans and mixed them with water, vanilla, and spices to make a chocolate drink. The Aztec name for this drink was *chocolatl*, and that's where the word *chocolate* comes from.

The meeting between Cortés and the Aztec emperor Montezuma in 1519

Left: Cocoa was a popular breakfast drink in the 1800s.

Below: An ad for cocoa from the 1920s

Cacao beans were so valuable that the Aztecs used them as money. They would exchange the beans for other things they needed, such as tools or cloth.

Spanish invaders, led by Hernán Cortés, arrived in Mexico in 1519. Cortés brought cacao beans and a recipe for the chocolate drink back to Spain. The Spaniards kept their new discovery a secret for about 100 years. Then, Queen Maria Theresa of Spain introduced the drink to her husband, King Louis XIV of France. He soon appointed a royal chocolate maker. News of the delicious drink gradually spread to the rest of Europe. It reached England in about 1650, and the first chocolate drinking house opened in London in 1657. By the 1700s, "chocolate houses" had become fashionable in England.

Chocolate was expensive in Europe at that time

Chocolate houses were popular places for people to meet and gossip in England during the 1700s and 1800s.

Left: Some chocolate products on display in a shop window in France

Below: An advertisement for chocolate

because it had to be imported from far away. It was a luxury that only rich people could afford. Smugglers began to bring cacao beans into Europe illegally. The smuggled cacao was sold more cheaply, so poorer people could afford to buy it. By 1850, Europeans had found that chocolate was good to eat as well as to drink.

People all over the world can now enjoy chocolate whenever they like, but a box of chocolates is still a special treat!

Where does chocolate come from?

Until the late 1800s, all of the world's cacao beans had to be shipped from South America, the only place where the beans grew. In 1879, however, some young cacao trees were planted in West Africa, where the climate is similar to South America's. The trees flourished, and by the early 1900s, many farmers in West Africa were growing cacao trees.

Nearly half the world's cacao beans are now grown in the countries of West Africa. The main producers are Ghana, Côte d'Ivoire, Nigeria, and

Cacao trees growing on the Caribbean island of Grenada

Sacks of dried cacao beans being loaded onto a ship at a dock in Brazil, ready to be exported

Cameroon. Cacao beans are also grown in other parts of Africa, Central and South America, the West Indies, and parts of Asia. Cacao trees only grow in the tropical regions near the equator, where there is hot sunshine and plenty of rain all year round.

About two million tons of cacao beans are produced each year. They are exported all over the world. The main importers are the United States and some countries of Western Europe.

Growing cacao trees

Some cacao trees are grown on large **plantations**. Others are grown on small farms. Farmers plant cacao seeds in **nursery beds** and carefully tend the seedlings until they are a few months old. They are then ready to be **transplanted**.

Cacao trees require heat, but they also need

Above: This cacao farmer, in Cameroon, is taking care of the seedlings in his nursery.

Opposite page: Young cacao trees are being shaded by taller trees on this plantation in Malaysia.

shade. Farmers may plant the seedlings near taller trees, such as coconut or banana trees. These trees provide food for the farmers' families and shade for the cacao trees.

A full-grown cacao tree is 20 to 35 feet tall. It does not bloom until it is four or five years old. Then, clusters of tiny flowers start to grow out of the trunk and branches of the tree. The flowers produce green **pods**. Cacao trees are **evergreens** that bloom all year long.

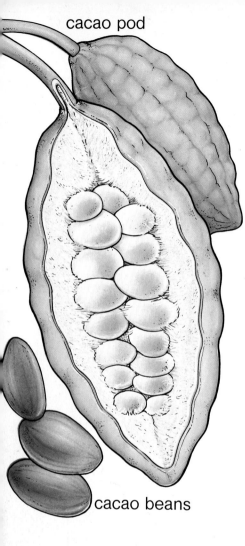

cacao pod

cacao beans

Harvesting cacao beans

Cacao pods take about five months to grow and ripen. A ripened pod is 6 to 10 inches long and its color changes from green to golden yellow or red as it grows.

The pods do not all ripen at the same time. It is very important to pick each pod at exactly the right moment. If one is picked before it is ripe or

Right: This Brazilian farmer is using a machete to harvest the ripe cacao pods.

Left: An opened cacao pod shows the beans and pulp inside.

Below: Cacao pods ripen at different times.

left to fall off the tree, the beans inside will not make good chocolate. During the harvesting season, farmers check their cacao trees regularly to find the ripe pods. They cut them from the trees with a long knife called a **machete**.

Farmers carry the ripe pods in baskets to a collection point. The pods are broken open with machetes, and the beans and pulp are scooped out. Each pod contains about 40 cream-colored beans surrounded by a white pulp. As soon as the pods are opened, air causes the beans to turn purple.

From farm to factory

This boy in Grenada is scooping out the insides of the harvested pods.

Cacao beans taken straight from the pod taste bitter and not at all like chocolate. The beans have to be **fermented** to bring out the chocolate flavor. When the beans and pulp have been scooped out of the pods, they are sometimes heaped onto banana leaves, then covered with more leaves. Other farmers may put the beans in boxes and cover them with wooden lids. The hot sun beats down on the piles of beans and their temperature rises, causing the beans to ferment. During fermentation, they turn from purple to brown.

After several days, the fermented beans are set to dry outside in the sun or indoors under hot-air blowers. Drying takes about 10 to 20 days.

When the beans are dry, the farmers and their workers put them into sacks, which are then loaded onto trucks. They are usually taken to

Left: The cacao beans are carefully spread out to dry in the sun.

Below: A government buying agent checks and weighs dried cacao beans in Malaysia.

the local agent who buys cacao beans for the government. Before paying the farmers, the agent weighs the beans and checks to make sure that they are good quality.

The sacks of beans are shipped all over the world. They will be made into cocoa powder or chocolate in the countries that buy them.

Making cocoa powder

Drinking chocolate being served by an 18th century waitress in Vienna, Austria

The next stop for the cacao beans is a chocolate factory. There, the sacks full of beans are **fumigated** to kill any insects that might be in the sacks. Next, the beans are cleaned and then roasted in large ovens. Roasting gives the beans an even better chocolate flavor.

The roasted beans are then passed through machines that crack the shells. In other machines, jets of air blow the bits of shell away from the center, or **nib**, of the bean. This process is called **winnowing**.

The nibs are put into another machine that grinds them into chocolate liquor. Part of the chocolate liquor is a rich, fatty substance called cocoa butter. This cocoa butter can be squeezed out of the chocolate liquor by machine. Removing the cocoa butter leaves a dry, round cake. This cake is then crushed and made into cocoa powder. Cocoa powder is used in baking and to make hot chocolate. The cocoa butter that is left over is saved. It will later be used in the production of chocolate.

Cocoa powder is packaged before being shipped to stores.

Making chocolate

cacao beans

cleaning

cracking

winnowing

grinding nibs

chocolate liquor

Chocolate is made from chocolate liquor with all the cocoa butter left in. If nothing is added to the chocolate liquor, the chocolate will be bitter. Bitter chocolate is used in baking. Chocolate liquor is mixed with sugar and extra cocoa butter to make dark chocolate. Milk chocolate is made the same way, except that powdered milk solids are added too.

These ingredients are mixed together and then passed through rollers to make a smooth paste.

The paste is put into a **conching** machine, which blends the ingredients thoroughly. Conching takes three days for dark chocolate and slightly less for milk chocolate.

Bars of chocolate are made by pouring liquid chocolate into molds. The chocolate-filled molds are cooled, and the chocolate hardens.

Liquid chocolate can also be poured over cookies and candies. Covering candies in this way is called **enrobing**. Some chocolates are made by putting a filling into a mold with a layer of chocolate already in it. More chocolate is then poured on top to cover the filling.

This diagram shows how chocolate is made.

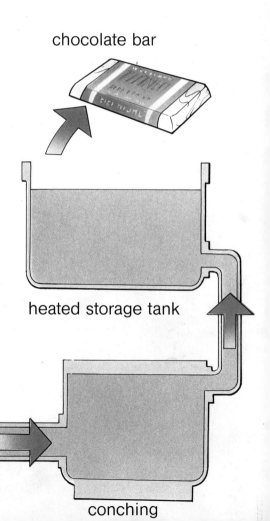

chocolate bar

heated storage tank

sugar

cocoa butter

grinding

conching

Chocolate and your body

Carbohydrates are foods that give us energy. Foods such as bread, potatoes, and sugar all contain types of carbohydrates. Chocolate contains sugar that the body can use to produce energy. Mountain climbers and soldiers often carry chocolate to give them instant energy when they need it.

The carbohydrates in chocolate and other

Chocolate is included in the Australian Army's survival kits.

Chocolate can help give people energy to run or play sports. Eating too much chocolate without exercising, however, can make us overweight.

sweets can be fattening if you don't use up the energy by exercising. It is unhealthy to be over-weight, so people have to watch how many sugary foods they eat. Too much sugar can also cause tooth decay. Brushing your teeth regularly helps stop tooth decay, but it is still best not to eat too many sweets.

Cooking with chocolate

Above: Cooking with chocolate can be fun.

What sort of food do you have for your birthday parties? Do you have chocolate brownies and cookies? Have you ever had a chocolate birthday cake? Chocolate is now an everyday food instead of the expensive luxury it once was, but it is still popular for special occasions. Cooks in almost all parts of the world use chocolate to make delicious cakes and desserts and to decorate a variety

Left: You can make all sorts of cake decorations from chocolate.

of foods.

If you've ever cooked with chocolate, you already know it melts when heated and hardens when cooled. This is not good if you are eating chocolate on a hot day, but it is useful when cooking with chocolate. You can melt it to pour on cookies and ice cream, or to use in baking your own treats. You can also mix it with powdered sugar to make cake frosting. Cocoa powder is used to flavor cakes and other baked goods.

Chocolate crispies

You will need:

4 ounces unsweetened chocolate

1 tablespoon butter

3 ounces cornflakes or other
   nonsweetened breakfast cereal

margarine

2. Remove the bowl from the heat. Stir the cereal into the melted chocolate. Make sure all the flakes are coated.

1. Put the chocolate and butter in a double boiler over medium heat. Stir until melted.

3. Grease some wax paper with margarine to keep the mixture from sticking.

4. Drop the mixture by spoonfuls on the wax paper. Put in the refrigerator until the chocolate has set.

Brownies

You will need:

1 stick of butter or margarine

4 ounces unsweetened chocolate, broken into pieces

1 cup sugar

1 cup flour

a pinch of salt

2 eggs, beaten

½ cup chopped walnuts (optional)

1-2 tablespoons milk

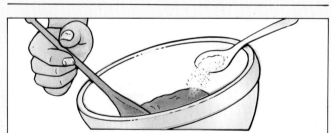

1. Put the butter and chocolate into a double boiler over medium heat. Stir until melted. Remove the bowl from the heat and stir in the sugar. Mix thoroughly and leave to cool.

2. Sift the flour and salt into a mixing bowl. Make a well, or hollow, in the center and pour in the chocolate mixture. Mix together.

3. Add the eggs and walnuts. Stir in the milk.

4. Grease an 8-inch square cake pan and pour the mixture in. Bake in the center of the oven at 350°F for about 30 minutes. Leave to cool, then cut into squares.

Chocolate cake

You will need:

1½ cups flour

1 teaspoon cream of tartar

½ teaspoon salt

1 cup sugar

1 stick butter or margarine

¾ cup milk

1 teaspoon vanilla extract

2 eggs

2 ounces unsweetened chocolate, melted

2. Sift the flour, cream of tartar, and salt into a bowl. Add the sugar, butter, milk, and vanilla extract. Mix together and beat well for two minutes. Add the eggs and chocolate. Beat for one minute.

1. Grease an 8-inch round cake pan with a bit of margarine. Make a circle of greased wax paper to line the bottom of the pan.

3. Pour the mixture into the pan. Bake in the center of the oven at 350°F for about 1¼ hours.

For the frosting:

1 stick butter
1 cup powdered sugar
4 ounces unsweetened chocolate
1 tablespoon milk

5. Break the chocolate into pieces. Put the chocolate and milk into a double boiler and melt over medium heat. Make sure an adult helps you with this part. Then stir the chocolate into the butter and powdered sugar.

4. Beat the butter until it is light and fluffy. Stir the powdered sugar into the butter.

6. Allow the cake to cool completely. Spread the frosting mixture over the top and down the sides of the cake. Smooth the frosting with a butter knife.

Glossary

cacao trees: the trees on which pods containing cacao beans grow

carbohydrates: substances in some foods that are an important source of energy

chocolate liquor: a mixture of ground cacao beans and cocoa butter that is the main ingredient in chocolate

cocoa butter: a fatty liquid that is released when cacao beans are ground

conching: the process of blending the ingredients in chocolate to make a completely smooth mixture

enrobing: covering candies by pouring liquid chocolate over them

evergreens: trees that bloom all year long

fermented: changed through heat, moisture, or an added ingredient

fumigated: cleaned, usually with smoke or gas

machete: a long, sharp knife that is used for cutting plants

nib: the center of a cacao bean

nursery beds: areas on farms or plantations that are specially set apart for growing seedlings

plantations: large farms where crops such as cacao trees are grown

pods: hard fruits of some plants, including cacao trees, that contain beans or seeds

transplanted: moved from one growing place, such as a nursery bed, to another

winnowing: the process of cleaning bits of shell away from the nib of a cacao bean after the shells have been cracked

Index

Africa, 10-11
Aztecs, 6-7

brownies, 4, 24, 27

cacao beans, 5, 6, 7, 9, 17
   growing, 10-11
   harvesting, 14-15
   fermenting, 16
cacao pods, 5, 13, 14-15, 16
cacao trees, 5, 6, 11, 15
   growing, 10, 12-13
cake frosting, 25, 29
candies, 4, 21
carbohydrates, 22-23
Central America, 6
chocolate cake, 4, 24, 25,
   28-29
chocolate crispies, 26
chocolate houses, 8
chocolate liquor, 5, 18, 20
chocolatl, 6

cocoa butter, 5, 18-19, 20
cocoa powder, 19, 25
conching, 20-21
cookies, 4, 21, 24, 25

dark chocolate, 4-5, 20, 21
drinking chocolate, 6, 7, 8, 9

enrobing, 21

ice cream, 4, 25
Incas, 6

Mexico, 6, 7
milk chocolate, 5, 20, 21

pulp, 15, 16

South America, 6
Spain, 7-8
sugar, 20, 22-23, 25

Photo acknowledgements

The photographs in this book were provided by: pp. 6, 9 (right), 17 (left), 19, Cadbury's Ltd; pp. 7 (both), 18, Mary Evans Picture Library; p. 8, WPL; pp. 9 (left), 15 (left), 22, 23, 24, 25, Topham Picture Library; pp. 10, 13, 15, 16, Hutchison; pp. 11, 14, ZEFA; pp. 12, 17 (right), Christine Osborne; cover, Peter Stiles.